Sherds of Merit

Poems by
David Hutchinson

Sherds of Merit
Poems by David Hutchinson
©2025 David Hutchinson

Publisher: Duncan Dobson

AMERICAN POETRY SYSTEMS
SOUTH SAN FRANCISCO
CALIFORNIA
"THE INDUSTRIAL CITY"

www.apsssf.com

APS#009
First Edition
9 7 5 3 1

Cover Photo and Art: D. Hutchinson
Cover Design: D. Dobson

ISBN 979-8-218-79504-7

Table of Contents

Foreword by the Author

Science and cosmology fascinate me, as do underlying histories and concepts found in nature. The exploration of how all of these coalesce in our lived experience under the backdrop of colonialism and etymology all the way back to antiquity then becomes the endeavor for me in shaping these pages. Often, it seems to me that in colonized cultures in which the native language undergoes a silencing, the oppressor incorporates ideas that originally came to fruition in that native language, incorporates those concepts into its own language, and then reintroduces them into the colonized society as having been invented by the oppressor himself. The examples of this, I believe, are many and represent a specific type of theft. So, in relying on etymology and multiple languages, the hope remains that while this work may at first appear alien or overly difficult, understanding every word or even the subject matter is not essential. I use tools, and even as the author I have forgotten what some of the words mean. The attempt remains to engender a response in the reader, from the often tragic to the hope of recognition of enduring beauty in this world we share with each other, and with our ghosts of memory.

So poetry can lend an uncertainty to all of this, and ideally an acceptance and even an admiration for the ambiguities of language and imagery in the modern, derived over centuries and regions: stolen, suppressed and elevated. Words lack much inherent meaning. They are bent by time, context and established vaguely by generations and morphology. Why not attempt to describe this in verse? Leave history, the word, as we go, and remember as we leave it on pages and footpaths.

So much of our languages is entirely dependent on context. Words may and do have many indications and the comprehension of them relies on the ways they are used and placed in proximity to each other in sentences, paragraphs and in the entirety of a given work. Much akin to quanta and wave functions, letters and words may function as singular particles but when implemented take on seemingly vast and unending implications.

The language here finds the page as at play within the intersections of art, nature and science, an embrace of the poetry we may find in watching a leaf fall to the ground and knowing that same tree shed leaves that our precursors saw descend similarly but on a different path, landing in eyes under circumstances we can ponder and linger over even as we watch it there on the ground waiting for a breeze to find it.

As perhaps a footnote, the cover photo is of a natural spring colliding with the San Francisco Bay. Moments prior, the bay won out and the pictured beach was awash in the waves. Would that these words, if read, similarly meet the mind of the reader.

David Hutchinson
San Francisco, California
September 2025

APS

For a friend who told me of generational trauma.
I was unaware. I feel the better for the knowing, and her.

Sherds of Merit

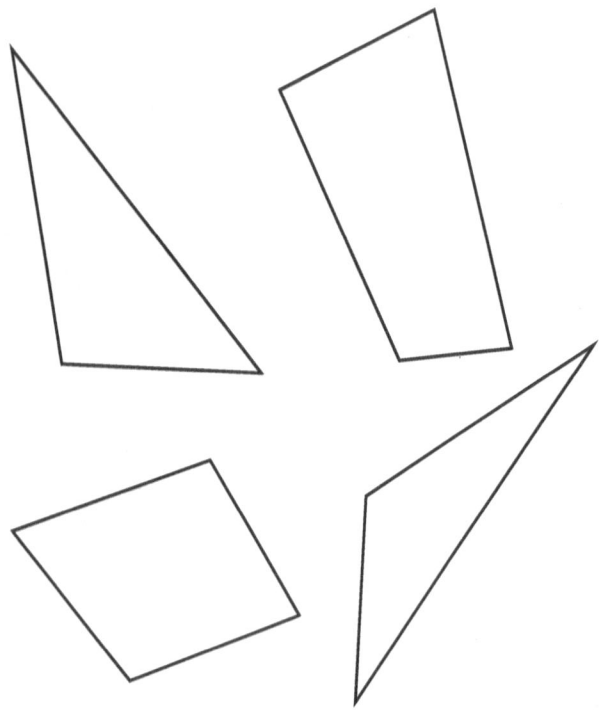

Sherds of Merit
A sea shanty of sorts.

Pliant coop in revel of a glimpsing host. Long dressed a sale of those persimmons busking. Street lobes crested by mummers hurling flexes, whelm for decent ballast. Birch the seep to shed enfolded. Cumber lots the polar braces bare; these are more than hollow.

Lean trough to beckon glow slants shade. A moresome after such heavel bands combed and splayed in half. Shaw to gather fronds undone or bunted under with episodal care. Equid sifters task a courser fabric furling. Chertish rifts of lucid funnels bestore the surface unders knapping for the rest. Pand else our very locks that festoon a burlish burdock. Lights avail; forged on blast since that no longer. Boulder up the wind toys and tincture oil motions. Egress dovers at the door.

Canon red all lapel names the fall face airing balls land soft as snow. Bent grass and dirt over gamble convents tense to vibrant frolics. Preen the hem fence hovel there, more than gone a rife. Ease a drift lazed serum; moan lee in labor granding stands of dated blooms that caught and stayed. Mingle goats evaporate in fog that blights and sunder sways a path to miss.

Mouth the cuts of vernal leaves all fasting to the brace. Faster crowns from plains afar robust and wither downs. Una hope to fly sogwil runers ground. Alwet and face that tool, to flame a torch of sight and sound and spray. Fare well posala, as the knoton wind winds up the hollow leaves. Atsila flags aboard a proper send that meets a listing latitude.

Word has it and a day of no other barber coils tight and flung ashore to heave and furl and gather. The mistral glares of glass give way to sand and mud and grass that waits to make a mark on those that walk and lie to look away each twilight and work the darkened trails.

Belest the limit. Hours conjure parasols of rang dull blossoms under fall. Call a bent, the sug wears fabling stores. The not tied tense by then besides fields of baleen. Under threaten that word or still the useful line to filter from the mind and corset mouths of cold and hungry tonnage. The look back long to take so fast that in dust reserved and rendered so to say. Know am the kaana laugh at frigid folly naked not unclothed approach before the sunder. Echo bogs of surging hunger under lingual torsions.

Canopy the bright angles fallen on a bloss; thes the writ of tort that weld the mild of penders relain or prone with peony. Hall aloud in quonal sleer the squander curlew. Aft aloft afar. Languish worders sleep to sing long replete that ample equan bears the monarch of airing wings that pattern duress skies. Arena sand contracts to tristad and bend the dirtish growth of sears and flesh that clash the shores of roaring umbrage and humble brags of smoke and fur. The knotted peony springs wide open to the sun and flights from color bare. Cold warmth to those closer to a sign tracing shapes in dark and light.

From entrañas to gloried victims that earl in the dawn asunder claps that strike a bone to chill a face full brunt of masted schools to linger catchment traps. Penned and ink a fence mapped only by the wave crest white to stellar grain. Ambival resins of foregone mosks ayelled and flint capped on impress reins to blind crossers. Replete cotton to the last.

Fool's gold ungent strikes that rupture bare and tower down and spread in creaks and dented spokes. Far lost differentials look out to agon burns that tumble forth in lumber words of recall. Edificial side notes circle fifths of hewns and branches unto eager reaches. Viber dawns cow before the sleep that comes with reps and leaps and blandings. A vagary recurs the scrape of hooves to ride a ship of constell gleem and light work. Oakum casks betend to feather instant relics of sleeping largess resting on a bed of tearing leaves behind a kind of kin known forgot to none.

Heartwood
For the redwoods.

In the forget

encased by a fear we were never meant to see because we
were not built for this.

That which took the time of all to rise
over tensile strength of forests.

A corporeal on an outside looking down
the length of years of undivide.
Born to reach that beyond
the form of formless remade to repel that life.

Pummeled under those that saw an opening
to the ground floor making way.
Over that barrel floated,
even while of the firm.

Upending that no end
of close to polls,

having felt the need,
without ability to bleed.

A lunge that split the air
asunder of assembly.
Monocular vision of a night
so fraught we no longer mourn.

Destoned in fragment mohs,
with teeth that fill the naked air
with clouds seen from a distant
beauty rising through a canopy of pain.

That tower of words
so uneasy to unfell.

The smallest in all the land
until rejoined in houses of a faction.

A vacancy evicted from Itself,
and a lonesome cellar remain.
Once a stellar reach become
that stunted and stale land born.

Littered with embers,
evident of the happened.
None but those who left can know
of how they went.

Gone they are before
they were even there.

Looked away so fast
from the forget to shoots.

Grasping Straw

Grasp, the plea for a release
from able to endure in pain.

The climb from pliet onto wings
beyond reaching vetch,
tendrils of ideas
in nested palate's rest.

Returns and opens,
on notions of the hold
within, and waits,

unbeckoned and welcome syllables
and roots on offered sounds
that sable flight has done so.

Oileán an Turtar

Turtle Island.

On the islands of the wind
astor petals spurred as wheels,
leaving reasons rown on gales.

Nascent collared mergansers
and migrations on the airs,
all that move and lift as flown
that might just find those there.

They are as many as the mist
that masks the light that runs,
yet scarce as solid ground
emerging from the suns.
Overturned beyond the husk
or all akimbo to the welkin,
that wight array of wisps
that gust above loose shores.

As the calm requites
and beckons whispered forms,
imagal efforts in the haze
and spheres yet to be born.

Ginger Mallow
On the pirate queen Grace O'Malley.

Sit in the dell and linger
over tea and primatur.

Tresses in hibiscus
over musty trods on bogs.

Galleys full and flaxen
rift forshore the circles round,

that caper pitching clarions
and stygian peat tar.

Plumed and basking face
of fearless scores unspoken,
sovereign and damp sails
into sheltered coves and eyots.

Exploits of forgotten journey
and visits with the grace
to return lost horizons
as the night befalls apace.

Set on blankets soft
or hard as awful years,
and drinks long left untoasted
growing cold on mantle tears.

The Fields

For all the young unpaid chimney sweeps.

In the fields of august creosote
that scape the wait of vines and folly,
early days spent head to amble overheard.
Rim the aksid underpass,
heedful keep the swallows.
Drafts below that sink the ground
in lonely narrow bellows.
Sweeps that coat
our orphaned buoys
adrift from crossings fraught.
Damper still that settled ash
and retains the will to rest.
For hold those blithful motes,
and burrows to the core.
They that rain the whinge
to drown our want to soar.

The Mounds at Vantage
On mound structures in history.

Clad in yarrow and the linens
of the poultice fleeced as downs
on standby to catch the tilter.
Patois picture window walls
up and oblique noblesse,
unwanted asks of early days
and have twos in the morns,
rex and cassia problematica and paleo
flies of furrowed towers locked
to constellations of the ground.

Outside the sackers roam
hectares hedged with limbless
trophies as inside sagitas
waits on annual light
to strike the channel passages.

Between the silence of omissions
and tribes unlost to voyents,
buried there as translators
the languished words between the parties,
in exchange for currencies of ferment
that flow from fertile fevers
as solar portals of the solstice
count the years inside released
by furtive yews that return to vaulted highs.

Surnames of the effete
shown no fear of discord,
only amalgams of accordance
in bedlam of the flock.
Seduced in earliest perfidy
in landscapes of the supernal,
the sprogs of know as told

resort to aching sword
of resolute avidity that climbs
or hunker down in ageless shell
among enduring tapered echoes.

The cons of piracy and wealth
in lieu of valued store in focative
aconitums, even as the credulous
sleeves of aqua 20ryngoes
emerge as autotrophs from lairs
to respire desperate arias
of exteriors and retreat
once more to seas
of circumnavigated fertility
that toil on unseen or parried.

Duals and tartan kidder screeds
of quoted marked dirigibles
and husbandries of crossed paths
over some left out
to second guess and watch
the chorus chant at odds
as enwreathed thespians
at play under canopies
and penumbras beyond the gambols.

The Salience

Append our days apart
from all that leaps and learns,
nestling on familiar frames
settled long in falling barns
of long-gone trampled hay
left scattered to the range.

No longer means to lift our cups
and pull from once we knew.
All ablauts without a cue
to share without the tense.

Known to many as the plains
as vast as days that never set,
only blend in softened dirt
of dormant miles walked while bent.

So many strikes that blunt the keen
and slice the waters
leaving wakes of torched diversion
bearing import to the wash.

So to take the leaves
from roundly shaken branches
almost touching ground
and shedding them stillborn.
Cinders made of locusts
descending from the skies
as clouds as thick as accents
and captured means to try.

Lingered over words
that simpler content made,
opposed to hollow scorn
and feinters crying might.

Thimbles

Long sinew and the risk
of shaping that bone to pull
through the eye.

Field dressed and an elegance
to dance away the tempo
and elope to distant greensward.

Such elaborate escort
that draws us muted to the yore,
we stiffen at the touch
so not to flow on tegument.

Worn proper as a hide
that safens in the drench,
inured above duress and salent.

Weaved in peril more than norra
engaged in labors long,
impaled as spiral daisies
growing short and strong.

The finery of our coats
and homogens to source,
patterns slayed of echoes
that dull to never find.

Embroidered over nail and ken,
no weight or clever signs,
to kneel and learn the songs
that teach how hard to press.

We sing them in our helmets
seldom heard beyond our ears,
free of concert rounds
or chorus voices bent,
outvied beyond the fears.

Gauze and Blankets

Allow that resound in canopies
of the flesh that hold our constellations' orbits
swirling within that shape us as we receive
the gazes from afar that reach us beyond light years
destroying time and distance to dance upon the waters.
These mortal wounds of never over
simply taken further form elsewhere and unknown
from before can't hurt enough of infinite
to make the difference known.
So we swim in these versions of embrace and recoil
our legs frantic in slow motion as the night
stars dance around us and we them their reflections
in confusion of the waves and for that long wet dance
of only moments we are just as them as us.

Intersectional

What does it mean to live between
the all but so alone
and with the lives
of bending time and fabrics still unsewn
by thought, and visions never seen.

Upwards of chapparal and giving way to treeline
and all that rises toward the sky
searching with defiance of directions.
Gravity of wait on the afternoon
of midnight's hours of the moment's never been
by ours, just the mystery of known.

To the Point

And we know sharp,
from the pierce.
The hue beside the cover,
drawn out at last in the shape
of side looks.
Numb from the ravine on down,
unceasing in relation.
A pier beset by the onslaught
overcome. Long enough
for the gull to ride the blade
on ragged wing tips
over vast and reaching plains
that only ever beckoned
soundless from above.
The descent unto the empty dust
that once rose in spinal descant strains.
That dive that sears the shorelines
of the midway broken.
Left to carry on.
Now exiled in a half shell
on the beach.

Kinship of the Mourning Dance

About Toypurina and Juana Briones, with shouts out to Zitkala Sa and the One Who Rasps.

Lot those who rasp the song and story
of embedded beams and cradles.
Sortilege of consanguine land, and sea
of ear to pole or tree.

They left from last wall bricks
of serpentine bemired,
quarried from above the forts and monuments,
and signatures split higher.
Revolt to counted acres over castile soap in mouths
or wrested silent domiciles.
The knowing urged by exile as a warning rise;
came in from toyon cures and hazel
to stand before recoiled onslaught.

Ire and purines spilled out in the dirty trials,
and ended in the walk away
to distant walled in gardens.
Hills of in between
as tending for the young,
on nights lain and aware
of bells and corridors so long.

Tyronic pyrimidines of the hurt spent ever in the warren,
calico and gunny sacks hung to a dangled roost.
Duumvir as engendered the well met
the neofita and the spent,
paired off to soldier on and more of those as sired
curanderas that arite the bones and commerce.

Cultivars in fertile valleys
so far from cattailed jaybirds
adorned with indigo,
acorn hoards and remedies
for the long and short and tired.

Wednesday's moss ground up in mortice
and saliva of the seekers,
hunkered now to whispers tuned
to catch the half asleep.

Those walking sticks and silver ducks
that strike on dowsers weeping,
batted lashes draw them in
to drown paced laughs of ruin.

Retch at repeats all of seasons missed
in the blur of labor's scorn
in dust, to try to hold the vanished;
promontory canines and dolor changed
into relief on shoreline bight.

The parted siblings rejoined as genrelation
matter teachers, passing on the blood of import;
slavered over as the bones of chicanery
and drunk as cowered wards,
steadfast imposition though
that know resort to allied sorts.

Off to altos green when the dominion sours,
astringent loam of profit gleams
ungrounded behind rowed bars
of grown in mono hues and stripes upon lone ports.

On sonoran antimony, stands brione above the hollow shade,
semblance of the communed to join

absent ever still alive.

Boughs to Loam

Charts to scrimmage draws
of fruitful paths in sight
with boughs to loam
to signal lodestars
of the sublunary
that invite the billows
to engender deluges
of this domain as arborials
from mycorrhizal embrace
to craft from careful in adroit,
expressed as fond
for consorts of the clement
and the leeway as a sway
in temperate embrace
of wellsprings in safe cradles
for the treasures as all neonates.

Three tankas

Wavecrest

Oldest waves are hills
crested to starlight oceans.
One treads on higher.
Correlates and cormorants
fly the spans and seasons all.

The Floating World

Often birds sing still
on branches' dancing in the wind
blown over oceans.
Flight silences want to chant
in lone pursuits of elsewhere.

Two Rivers

Two rivers and the same
one rapid and one slower
reach the bay in time.
The mouth in motion of claim
speaks both in ever due course.

Means to the Winnow
On language.

On potential for the weight of words
that descend as aeronomies
within the argots of allegiance
betwixt the fathoms
any organ may portend.

Faculties on the usury in petrified
propalis, or the cyrus of diplomacy
and anabasis xenotypes
or zaptiehs, at play on arches for the fauna,
our latencies as manifest
as paramita within primata.

All sagacities in motion
with derivations on abounds
to destinations of arrivals
as salutations in return.

Pestles for the vivified
floes to glaciatic deliquesce,
inebriated by a certain pram
delivered as the glyph
over retributions in the bygones
hovered as two allied eidilons in ether
strained by constant exerts
both cerebral sonatas as corporeal.

Sorts of spaldas joined
as consents of the aegis
provided here in tranquil faith
to steer us on expedience
from the shambles to the lucid
whits of focus in alacrity.

The mutual intents of lector
with the listener, unfurled
to horizons on the natch
mentored by the gifts
flown to linger in the study,
never fumed by dismal pipes, but circulated
on long ladders
by carbonic protos in primordials
arisen in slow to simmer pyrolic
creatives of discernment
shared as gentle genuine accord.

The Face of the Earth

To look with listen at polarities' blankful face,
from afar so near to sea
the pounding of the years.

A desert then but not before
having lived all lives not as reward
for surging climbs and distant depths
that drown the views
in weaker visions of forget.

Waves on then and still some more
to teach with time some unheard sound.

Masks dissolved in leaning
curvatures of before,
each one in perceived shells that round
more tears of lost yet gifted graves.

Race on to never ends
these moments still remembered
as they viewed, even as they
caught the next, by agreed to never rest.

Quench

Probably there will be the
effort of tension reached
slower and below quench.

Stone's Thrower
For a cavewoman.

Denticulate tools and taxon tales of how we arrived
from so many early stones thrown for survival at altar
or plateaus south where eruptions in lakes of fire
still slow the veins and soon require furs be worn
to fight the frisson of the freeze
in futures delivered more a boulder.

Particles of a melting icicle
divided only by the moments and our need
to know by separation the arcs of years' entirety
when contrivance knapped for flame or kill
give way to form of amulet or idol then on to steeple's chase
and towers looming over believers as subsuns
and parhelias that shatter skies above
advance our creation withdrawn into caves to hide
and draw beliefs and sing the songs of worship that reverberate
off walls as sonic histories escaped from hibernation and echoed
actions.

Two spirits shedding skin while the hunter in the exoskeletal
skull with molars of a sort pair with larval bearers
and on and 'neath the surface the heavy machinery of the orb
moves the earth and pollinates the cycles
and fish eats midge and cicada sleeps only to wake
and hide the heavens once again with density and obscured
clouds that deluge the land in floods of breath.
Survivals of the distance arrived here from long past still
but resemble hooven goats scaling edifice in search of licks on
salt.

Ovens in the dens of time and these names mean naught to
them or us
but that the early dies of repetition and the current follows
with its own exploits as told or writ on rocks again
to be read by those who seek to know but can't

as these artifacts and fragments tell only stories
and have freed that life force flown away so long ago
and that oddly crooked finger bone that just hooks
imaginations to the fear of living amidst the time when
simply existing was the way but soon the rocks and walls
themselves became the stuff of faith that held us safe from
harm, or kept us out because we were born only to believe but
search.

A Semblance

Intimations just from the former
brought hithers' insincere
by hunters for themselves
lost long ago to incarnations.

An understand awry
of patterns and random tendency
leaning into headwinds'
beliefs that the self the sole unto.

With blinders either side
buffeting the vision
that all are justly capable
the same as help or hindrance.

Endurance adopting care
for the wayward and the strength
alike in that they stand alone
at either ends of lakes.

Bridges in between
sometimes are deftly built
defying distance and aversion
to share as mise en placed.

Some refuse to look
or even contemplate
that all of vastness capable
and far differently escaped.

From the drudgery
of only perceiving from afar
the oppositions of embrace
that lift our minds beyond.

The limits that bind
as connected to the space
the fortunate to find
all that so interlaced.

Lattices of concern
for the company enduring
without regard for that the same
offered as best in return.

Climbing vines that free
to drift on winds of lost
to finally reside there
pollinating without regret.

For that so left from where
once the germinated born
allowed to recall with compassion
both the celebrated and the sore.

Missed and not forgotten
that all had played a part
of vitality and valued
for some and hopeful more.

Areae

Camphor in the night churn
of cells and oblast locomotive
wind sore isms and the tangor
embossed palmar hoar, and surgeon
luce the carbuncles in mercer.

Balms and bridgeheads held at odds
with remote limekiln pressors
and glass bead curtains
of bowling greens and beggars
to the columns of the debarred
raw and gummatous in reverse
cathay sylphs of deserted gratis
to the oscitant skits of ulcer.

Four winds though of fey
still on just deeded mardier,
as passé on gladden parables
and piebald forms of arar
with affiliates and peerless aborns.

Nor the distant supplants, on hiatus
from the confronts never sated
simply gams with miles of cover.
Redress through the ageless
that overcome caudillos of allurement
and suborn to wring the reaps
on thrall of vertebral pilasters
under duress from the trifles.

Still the myriads of largess
brought to bear the duplex
of the minion, and await untold accouchements
of the kindred animas
adrift along narrow passages
of furrowed worth and clemency.

Ashes to aes

On a flood, rivers, and fertility.

Versions of a leonides wrought
to origens of atonement's ash
and turns about of long fast midas' clash
with mercantiles and visionaries slaught
for phaedra's io whites
and singing gadflies hovered over bahr al nil.

Eastern suzerains' adopted helpmeets
and vessels wielding only fibulae
to gift the scarves of dulband in gordion,
and the labial spectrums realized
over tumulus walls of phrygians' demise,
as then overturned in foulkons of the keratin
formations, under duress from said xiphos
on down the passages to accelerants and ore.

Di mons of leonidas' forelocks and shields
in golden sands of pactolus flows to silenus.
Hearers hidden from the sight
with fabrics wounded over faint inscriptions,
theories heard and said aloud
in trinite cups of mythos light.

Sapphire stones and blue tassels
on tablets of the brit,
decisions of the scythes and hourglasses
that call from hollowed horns
to sauls beside the gallups overwrit.

Convenants of the da and right
to dynastic stipulations' promise
lines acceased to follow that close fragrance
touched by agonic commons of the diverse,
mistook for plasma modes of falciparum
commends comuns plets and weal,

the publicums pro to wedjebten, neith and iput.
Spirited and swathed, floating reeds as transom
forth the first of sargon's chairs and choirs
in the forks and eddies tied,
as interlocutors of the bodies' waters
be they bogazi, zaire or yazoo rides on mians.

Pastaza basins of equivalences' spring,
synaesthesias of remembrance' forwards
in shifting derivations of arrivals as estranged
by concurring alchemies of tragicom.

Obsidian delivered on velar u's and afterclaps,
the metallurgies' shifting chains
on axelic roads beyond nevsehir-nigde's overlaps.
Spent centum battling satum, mercies plowing andecite
below ceramic anatoles sung to glotallic bowls
in logico laws of soundings echoed, chambered,
be they the prisons of marches' legendaires expired
or downward shafts that rid the nights
of denrinkuyu mornings left
to depicted axo's carnage.

Seconds of cappadocian repeaters,
from melendiz brooks slaking thirsts of brahma
on the banks of sprawling asikli hoyuk
over to the dwelling denisovans at xianjiang
in the zeguo lands abounding on chang jiang
cold fronts from above evenk loanesi
climes that suggest worn leaves of death
in warmth from that which doth provide us.

Eisegesis of nomadic swirls in trouses
and by on mares to riders both,
the pastoral plains of actions' speech
that forms the fibrous lapses
on looms of antiquated threads to otzi
and return as conflictions of zarshayamna
to breech the bindings for synapses.

As heard in nag hammadi to the copts,
or before as synecdoche of noenum
to quelle source asunder be there none.
Scrolls of discourse un to bear for amenmesse,
split in tombs from those left there
with tia, siptah and takhat,
merenptah realms as faded way to hyksos'
subjects as the rule of turmoil
in the halves to crescents of deserted.

Excavations of the pasts
wrought with queries of the unasked
for impositions in hemispherics'
ease, defended as a limestone
brick and answers' masked euphorics.

Exiles of typteined skins awander,
retaining anointed gifts of guile
in crafts of adrift on the waters of esikongo,
or upstreamed from aha kwahwat projectiles
sent from atlatls of nahuatl, touched
not ever by those stark tags played by steorfan.

Rythmics of percussive stables read by planisheres,
these daylight revolutions of the quaternary
shortened, to meet the tides as gnomon cast
in cratered mal'ta buret withins
of upheavals' risen on andean breasts
pulled skyward on condor wings above
to give anthropos' of magneto rest.

Age of nary promises of the artistries of try,
manweso glauco ever younger flies
even as noctua dusk in ninevah reborn.
Triage the terms of geagnian again or geldane
wards' adopted gowns thrumming
the following of horus in festivals of red boats of seth
and buto until sanakhte returns from hoards

of buried turquoise and guggelsterone
in punt to excite the senses to electrum.

Auditory adit swims to floras' rejuvinated
furtherance as censored grids
on cobalt obelisks, known to be tablet
lists of cardiacs' adjacent feathers
fanning forth back to return by current days
assumptions in entwined agrarians
of archipelagos oceanic around pangaea
as descriptors above the interglacial
but within those parametric codons of evolit
to the gloried inanna's tender margins.

Usurped from the abodals refined by everlasts
for calls to arms for lilitu lifting anzu,
within the empty conch shells' undulations'
spiral, far out over the wider seas departed.
Sprouted forth from holanikus of ubiquity
across the spectrums in festivals' antiquity
the sacral crann bethadhs be of nilotic lotus
combs wielded in dated palms of kemet
under asvatthas' united in the meditations
metu neter reverberated by the bells and songs
that dance from face to face as creases just as strong.

Gulfs among the nyx and circular seals of uruk
submerged in annals lost to adytons
where tympanons and chorus stomps
in mysts of phanes, to edge the feathers of the aether
sending tsunamics of bended articulations
that dive for tridents' distant desmid,
twofolds of bilgames' fins of versatility
and eternal modernic enkidus so volatile.

Wild consorts in ecstatic prologue's deluge
erupted by the gapes of tarturus unseen
to bifurcations not of civility's genrelations

but absolved as convenient certainty
of threaded nahyati cast by rising sawel.

Demis perseid and leonid showers entwined
with recurring geminids that rain,
to precipitate the bringers of the praxis
solidified, and celebrate on walls' immure
that may release transcibed fonts'
capacities to altars' that nourish both thygaters
and solar flares of each thespiae and leuk as bher
of mirus to flourish in cyclic resolutions' krene ghel,
manifolded by the neo dhes of placers
kere that sink the sands of gobleki tepe
in resurgent canaliculi of wodors of barsans
to bhel below horizons.

Hemispheres

Though aristarchus may be clear
to equations in the ether,
not so from marianas dwellers
in the phosphorous' own light.

Gone but to the afterlight
of remembrance born
by reflections from above
that revolve walking on either.

Just reflections in the distance
of that desire sees
be that weakness in a difference
or thoughtful generous solidarity.

The light soon reaches
even arctic skies
in luminosity of springtime
that washes driftwood from the beaches.

Southlands bathed in long shadows
of alerce climbing ever high
along the coasts to canopies
and towering embrace of distinction.

Qualms that linger on refrains
still echoed from the past
that offers naught but doors
unopened wherein we deposit the gains.

Midpoints shifted as borders
of relinquish, geographies of establish
that present the image of agreement
as temporal as entreaties in two scripts.

One that's just as written
and another misunderstood
as the story of lives lived
with an empty claim of always could've.

Pagus

Believe the leaves that sway,
from far off distant meadows'

gravity

of artemis in stride,
to return the gaze of leonids

as, soon as,

the morning beckons,
all the pleasant nights.

Echo Lake

Under volume flows the weight that speaks
with tongues on wind
or desolated fields of granite
and gravity of effort
simply there for both.

The whits of in between and walking cairns
that pique the follow before the tumble
shatter the apprehension unfolded
to approaching the mountain
by the drinks of rivers.

Returns of wigeons along the marsh
of slow elevation building
shadowy borders of no definitions
and fading light on the undersides
of translucent waves of clarity
and the shallows of deception
or what became of asia major

that better give us all that to create
the motions found in that these
bottomless lakes so akin to each
remind of vast depths of being
that connect us as we travel.

Enjambment

A river unends
in seas or mountains rising
to carry bird flight.

Over that or far below
the view obscured in distance.

Wherewithal

Withal heron sounds without a song,
just the thrumming of such spans
that threaten nearly to displace refrains.

Their eclipses falling down
to blind all that below to deaf
not noticed as they fly on to nest
in trees leaning on their burden.

Yet still a branch unperched
by diminutions of the arctic tern's
in body but mighty of the wing
to take on that challenge
to release the tree of necessity
and let it sing the unheard melodies
in wind and billow forth on updrafts
south to repeat the lessons learned again.

The Startling

For a hawk, a squirrel and dog.

Shouldered of the branches
as the sights of correspondence play
in drifts on a calamus of semblance
to apprise the restful tributary,
balanced for then alofted,

and on along to furs on ceded terrain forewarned
in the choreography of leaves on downdrafts,
both that hold, or fan, the wind
of that as gesture to alight near peril,
a frailness behind an arch unseeing,
the aged canis,

ever coursing fleet of foot on meadow
succumbs to feints
supplied by jaegers up above
to the cupule hoarders
that turn tail in opposing and reverse
of canopies and atmospheres below
the confusions of the exquisite
as a favor for the forest.

The Skeleton Crew

So few as to be counted,
on figures leant on air by effort
from before.

Analemma bared from passage
on the habits,
that gleam to skyward tern.

Wingbeats all our motions
tho just 'neath the surface' stares
that hold prey,
still moving,

far, hushed, yearned.

Offered up to by gifts
freed from reward;
a dram of ocean covered,
in blinks
from standing light.

The Patience

A vertigo in light
that orbits far above,
no longer seen as clearly
as that lonely flying dove.

In the waiting room for triage
to assay the needs' dismay,
how can there be so many
and how far can they stay.

The fragilities of discourse
enveloped with a seal,
swimming so far in distance'
source that words cannot explain.

To never find the beauty
of watching only still lives
staring always seeing
the fog come in to blur.

Quilted downs and feathers
scattered all about,
asking questions of the bodies
and the whethers of return.

So in the bay of wolves
always at the lunacy,
of flight on wings aplenty, and to tarry,
on the tranquility of solve.

Loved with the arms around
the circumference of ellipses,
the etceteras as stung
by listening with the sound.

Climbing ladders to ring bells
to bring the parties near
enough to know the joy
that all of us may hear.

Refuse

Gathered in the spaces
between the lines of furrowed want,
the eyes that see
across the crowded closet
the fellow travelers to gaunt.

Shared as burning drums
that fill the lands with discard
debtedness of built but not erected
for the habitation of the keyless
search for hope and all the more ejected.

Shambling down the years
of the debris of worthy
of the simplest glance of notice
and the knowing in acknowledge
to walk behind or far ahead.

Still holding out for lack of better
the hope none must in solitude
line the trials and the fears
but with cognition taught and learned
that enlight appears only in such motive.

All can be addressed as egalite
just in a place that's obscure
from all that lay between
to deter mutual humanity
from rising choirs singing joys for free.

Pallor

Dearth of capes and horns that gore
hope for what might have been
and leave just staggering
cities that still rise above the foothills
that they themselves razed
in the shelfless constancies of search.

So the only rest becomes the final one
and that perception in the moment
amounts to the always said and done.
Round but oblong coins
found in the dirt but bent
by time and friction that recognizes
the faces of our history's distortions
remade in the hallways of the mirrors
reflecting light upon us
plainly as some unasked-for curse.

Some ebonic plague of forethought iterations
to combat within revolving waves of spin
that provide solutions to endemic hate
through ferocity of hunting chasers
bravely standing in the frays of those created
wars for profit that have eroded bullets
down to musket balls or crossbows
by hides in return, akin to growlers
that cannot be seen to sin outright
but only rend and bring to tears
all futile efforts that hold no risk to them.

So on the march the months of panic
given over to slow declines of hills
once rich with established egality
that flies as eagles do above the winds
of months in passing ever to arrive
unnoticed as the dirt below drinking

the red rain of loss without an end
until there lands between the tides
of caribe on the land of mountains rising
the knowledge the wars but not against
but only that we don't succumb to avarice
and the icing of guts inside and out
by lofty butterflies and stolen freedom from afar,
verily rebel against those visage stamped papers
and always game up for the fight,
chasseurs rose up to claim their due for all
from a distance that shape us as
our own device that assumes a bettor
on unjust accounts still paid in reparations
to this day of not forgiven,
be kept by surf strates of the body
but the embraced perception that occurs
in the resistant arts of beauty
and the mutual equal open books of mind.

Broken Axle

Bone structures of a halvened strake,
strewn in driest prairies of abandoned
ivory skull and horns not far away,
and scrimshawed by the storms
of dusted desperation and starved rocks,
the cliffs that leave no trace of shade below.

Driven foreheads left to deserts' promise
of empty days between the cuffs,
the gears careening in expanded girth
of rawhide whips to release
the scorched burns of screaming breaks.

Motions of the gathered to welcome
railing fences, undone to further discourse
from betterments of worth the pauses
from the journeys all so longs
in coaches pulled by motives of locale,
to end so soon for the densest ores
to hide from endless breakers' clouds
singing matters to the distant bluffs.

Escarpment

On Starved Rock for those who vanished there.

Fault lies just as found,
rising on trust in mindful balance.
Edges vanish far below,
sound reaches there unheard
to those standing up on high
shouting out the word precarious.

So steep to starve the rock of leaves
in the seasons of attrition,
the growing frailness out there
bearing witness without mercy
to the side trips of the tourist watching
choices loom, themselves to turn and wait.

Land bridges to an holm
only reached by long desire,
out there to face the returning sun
that circling orb the only fire.

Still, welcome in the morning
but not to those on continent,
the waiting game
to render rock
entirely sea bound.

Alone then finally
staring back at the glisteners,
bereft of even longing
for the vanished from before.

No reasons left to want
so sitting knitting songs
of transparencies and apparitions
until those also are gone.

By the moment for release has come
no more there to save,
flown into the sky
to fly among the brave.

Half House

Dusted shingles of a steep slope
secured by hard links
tethered to a hemp rope.

Rows of cloudy clothes
drift by as rain falls
heavy on the frames
of stolen promise
left cheaply shod and hobbled.

A noble ovis aries
for the fleecer worn,
the lid to follow
from the knell
that countless others harmed.

Plenary from the welfare
tho no risk to baas we swore,
given all the want
a call for scarce and pallor.

Swathed in textile thorns
all among the bare foothill,
erect in tenon, joined of assembly.

That pale house on the hill
born of brothels for the lorn,
on doleful deltas and long dead
pines of floating spates
to harvest orchards
over engulfing seaboards.

Caricatures
On Oscar Goodbar Johnston.

On stages left abandoned behind
speeches' empty loud
the ghosts of imposition
reside elsewhere,
deaf to sounds
of hearing knot
that binds our knowing to us,
in the wings recanting
lines read behest of intermission.

Delta of a fertile land
first removed and then of import
to export pain and grinding,
the toils' unrelenting bent
by sun and hurricanes.
Then conflict between compeers
on the enmity of gelt
to reconstruct but as the mere veneer
of photographs of progress cropped
not shared or even shallow
but smoking breath of acrid acrimony.

Looming tillage of those seen less so
by gins of separation
in threads of nevermore
and betum leaves in flues
that cure to ill
and ailing animus
or forced embrace of iron
and the lungs' false renditions.

So the decades pass left out
of bargains not collected
just the exploits of the few
in depressions of the ticker tape

paraded in cells of singularity
indentured to the labored statues
of malfeasance tilthing the soil
of stripes on drums of poison
cidere never sated
simply obscured by thickened pineland.

Searchlight

Communiques, so many of the letters
as gambles of conveyance spent
and then again or else than not,
mining rocks for holes in pockets
torn for far too long
and given over to the laundry,
not for darning but distant maintenance
on cold solace of the night
in towns empty of worship songs
just ledgers of the even scores
in smart illiterations of the pathfinders
whose names get lost to books
designed as shambolic contradictions
of love for singing grass, not betters shaped
on the winds of sailor's shorey lifting
off to hurl the debts of temple toggles
deep into those that always knew
to dive to depths beyond electrified
but far too late to die,
and always too much to lose.

Surround that cape not round but draped
in bronze eternals of self-made
to celebrate the victories of loss
that spill on to pages on parade,
the parables of who man and she
on claims staked with destiny at play,
as one but staggered still lingers
ever longing for naat' annii
among the ursus and the bison
for miles split by vitulum and long walks,
so welcome the daunting weight
of years of yester released as quills of hope
for sudden commonalities elapsed,
the dawning ink wells of mutuality.

Ballad of Moses Rose

On the so-called yellow rose of Texas.

From the rear of drawn line,
through window in the pitch
piercing the opposed as column
to counsel waiting descent.

Awful chorus on repeat of fables
of the ancestry invented to defame,
inaptly named by years alive
and a craven bloom of shame.

Not a sheila of the lee and coward hue
this enlisted so renown,
for the battles enjoined
from campaigns back to rushes complex.

A lyric altered for prosperity
unlost in lingered scorn,
propriety of lies and disparition
for no better part of valour.

Fast besieged and overrun
by repute of revisions dreamt
the intrepid as released
appraised alone and long unkempt.

Alarm bells for deserted grass
and plasma spills at night,
those stars fall onto skies
well lit by candle light.

To scribe notions of heroes
and the tombs as told,
but rarely right as victors
that can't grow to be old.

Betrayals in the vanished chronicle
seen through lenses as a smear
of dark third months of siege
and gusting santa ana fables.

Blossoms now besmirched
just as the many sisters
all befuddled stories known
from charlatans on trophies perched.

Those dry heat rocking desert porches
where blame's assigned as diamonds,
the starry skies before the crude retreats
erupted up into forevermore.

Banjos plucked by fabricators
and country miles of cheap mansions
on hills without a view
just fire ant mounds and laughing gators.

Sun belts seen as gallantry
and exotic produce by supremes,
self-described as such by faithless warrants
to oppress, elected only to believe.

Carried

Rutless with the vigilance ahead,
awaits on long breath under shade of tree,
as if not there, the strength.

Those that flew on broadbacks
or within obscura skies for miles
only to be torched, for their.

The murders of the corvids mortal,
with detritus delivered
and caws the breath
to rise and stand
for rush to meet
that arrives with song,
to with an ease
walk away
in concert.

The Earlier

On a moat in the park.

That outcropping so revered
as source for craft and sustenance
with concurrent fires to keep the company,
rising within an ancient seep encircled
and bridge to quarried from chert red folded,
not to protect as had been the custom
for ageless aeons of two lands
but kept from in tragic display
of present but not for now,
between a lake without a boat
for those who turn to knapping glass
or forgotten altogether
as fragmented as the shards
hurtling through the airs of past.

Might we regain our lost to all the lands
that held us as a people,
who over all the battles
retain ourselves and still,
come to revive from the extant word,
that still exists as dialect
of a'ho for that simplicity
so vast in the enduring beauty
we know as nature.

Cataract to Spit

In solidarity with a poet's name and hopes for an end to war in Ukraine.

Landlocked by the sun's invite
on the water's rush
down all the canyons of creative
and the gravity
of yesterday.

Aedein's listener singing in the fields
hears by looking in both eyes
and gliding through the calm
embrace of the turbulence of dear.

Who could have seen and never stopped
by formations of lust's designs,
but laid on beaches breathing
the gently lapping waves
and warmth upon the skin.

We share the visions as have seen
both then just as before
the water's edges gone
to blur and cascade's dawns.

Difference of peninsulas to islands
or days' gives way to nights,
none as spoken honestly
with heart's traditions free of divisions
from the sand floating on the rafts
and lifted spirits
and fears of remembrance
as celebrations' living remains.

Suffer not them
but justice lost
to hollows and deep shade,
knowing still that grows there

a sprouted peace emerging.

So in our beds we sleep
in the flowers of our tears
knowing we won't forget
or ever be the same.

.

.

Tontine

The last to rest here undone by wait
for such to befall,
the remainder of the swimming pool
of tontine become only all too clear.

Each one a ledger all to the own
living absent fear,
of investment or loss of principle
without ethics freed of language.

Incentives become ever more dire
to eliminate the debts,
of bodies born so long ago
the value receded into anguish.

Fear of involvement after the fact
there're prices paid,
not for living well but solely dying
over distant shrinking clubs.

Paid in growing interest of the pact
that may appear as lack,
one and another missed as mark
and the remaining rewarded in the crying.

Possibly but not always certain
some may be just gone,
none to share the beautious of life
but the last to perish into the dark.

In Clemency

Bygone trails long left unwalked
that lead to nowhere's destinations,

on either side of weedy paths
scorched by the sun of years'
intentions and wayward necessity
gone fallow but not replenished
to spring to life's new seeds.

Dormant still but covered under
lay the sources there, waiting
free and boundless
as the seasons march across
much wider vistas' lengths

leaving untrod and not tamped down
or mined, but loosely shaped as earth.

Nestled

A word uttered, what,
follows bygones of ours.

That sound of tears

and streams encumbered
by almost.

Toy Sail

Flat jigsawed hull shaped wood
with mast and sail of bush leaf
stuck tightly into hole drilled
for the motion but sent only
on the current of hope by

its maker following faster
along the wet and sandy bank.

All the way to sea the game
and not deterred by eddy
into run aground on obstacle
in creek or fragile island

for a while until bored
and dry shoed and far too old

for this but still somehow
unable to abandon each
in crafting yet one more
in that garage that never left

without these lingered dreams
of all that came before to comfort

in despair of youth that never
can a body be truly all alone.

The Portal
For San Francisco.

Halved by turbulence of surges
that circumference of and in the window,
first seen from a second
party, from yon hill above pacifica.

Those there and not waiting
or cold from elements,
inviting unto the lands
to warming huts and yerba buena.

To be received yet shunned
and on to future ventures
of animosity in vigilance
and wealth of frantic desire.

So a fort arose
and not far from the bay
but unbaked adobe walls
in the fog of never close.

The toil never ceases
to offer efforts without reward
just the lasting burdens
of fear and unsung lives.

All in the confines' prison
of either guarded keep
or flock, the denizens of early days
and dwindling larders to be stocked.

Conflagrations of such magnitude
that gaslight transformed to lightening
and mighty rivers cease to flow
to trickles any time of day or night.

Expositions of renown that draw
from far and wide to celebrate the ages
of modernity as past achievements
and their failures lost to the mists of excess.

The disappearance in the dunes
to the gardens of the western lands
out to amusements' statues
staring at the flames of all antiquity.

Down the halls of bustling streets
in the rising shadows of ever taller
conceived as spans and mighty constructs
of two banks and furthest waters met.

Deltas flowing through the reeds
to push the tide away
past the skylines built on abandon
up to the foothills of the fortunes.

Modest gains of bouillon tradewinds
that leave some floundering and stalled
as anchored to the mast or many clubs
that protect the wanton and alone.

Jumped ship for the fields
of sierra loads that call to come
to suffer winter's frigid climes
to wait for dirt lettuce' spring again.

Returned to hothouse and the dens of thieves
to lose it all and start again
to sleep it off unknowing
and wake aboard once more.

Current lines of flooding rivers
at full tilt and swirling round the bends,

these breeches of ages are all but not gentle
rarifications of eponymous straights ashore.

Hills as overlooks to glimpse
the vastness of such waters and sands
of stretching lands themselves rising
and falling harmonies much as waves below.

Persistent without the rigid forms of east
these pacific gems of welcome sun
and wind and rolling clouds of density
enveloping the city grand in reliefs of gray.

Reached by land from peninsula
trails or continental tracks or longer
even round the hope and for years
the square-rigged sail right past.

Waves of arrivals and departures
whether jumped the ship left
to fill abandoned wetlands and sleepless
bars so dark to wake up back on deck.

Always the resupply to carry forth the sums
for gentry and the class to grow exclusive
and for some to maintain unrest of labor
put down with the forces of divisions' loss.

As derived from placer and removal
but to whom appeasement given
well asked as before the larger looming
reasons all that's set aside in service of accrual.

Destined to remain the holdout
of mercies' great conferrals on those
who set forth here on the ships of many
to hear the horn and light that signal welcome.

Scuttled

A boat scuttled by a gale
has discovered an island,

and has become,
assured as the sand.

Later to appear in tourist pictures
in foreign countries

or as backgrounds

in the shiny grains
of fashion magazines
thumbed through from tables.

On Tanglefoot

By the piles of seagrass sweating flies
lay a broken brow once holding,
so became just but a shell
no longer marching with a swagger,

or telling lies to half truths in their ears
but presenting them for all to see,
on a beach called end of years.

The drinking salt waits as a table,
calving particles aplenty,
their taste but just a flavored dagger
of poverty masked as chicory.

Cut with icy hail and conviction to make pleas,
from those left staring down
at skulls in tanglefoot's long misery.

Beached Elk

On an elk laying in the rocks with a broken back on
the Lost Coast waiting for the tide.

On that day stood out a tongue

in words all but unknown.

The tool employed
a diver's glossary
of silence as adopted.

To harbour all the ruts and roads
that present the want of worship,

the fall that ended on the bluffs
flows in rivers salted.

Mercy given as guts to punish
the rocks on which we lay,
our backs that break upon us
in this our long foray.

Rest a hail between two passages
and in between a wayward strand.

The hart that beats on as tide,
or story left undone.

And looked upon the speech
of those who've reached impasse,
if recall serves no more
the waters remind for all.

Those who continue on
up the beach ahead,
and other paths to fortune,
of waits, and thirsting thoughts and dread.

From there the eyes of many
look in upon the trees,

an invite to a swimless slog
that may exult, in the run up to the flying.

Geswin

Melody all song, silent neck out
as sakes of appearance

or domecilic visit
still extant from nonexistant.

Pidgin holed
and so what might their tongues say.

Name any as they please
to refuse an overture of a song

out loud, and ever more.

Eutropia
For a friend on the bus speaking language.

And each unto pluralities of verse
that rain around as farisi gaits,
symboltaneous touching ungrounded motion
and all fluencies
landing those within the oceans of so many thoughts
aswirl in sudden bios on acoustics
running ever onward from before and back ahead,
lifting, rearing toward the drifted nurse.

By all that hear the light of words
spun audibly without direction
until arrival among the ears
and gathered, to listen as some
presently among,
if not pleasant, around enough.

Influences of gradients freed of meaning
whether cells or stars be they
in confluence of aperture circumspected by own gravitates.
In that orbital of life and well met strangers
aware of both more and less
these rides that never end but change
carry hope not overcome or desperate pleas
but pleasant greats that pass as friends
we cannot know but enjoy all just the same.

Not blinders lead us hither
we run just where we may
the paths to follow leapt as trails in falling rain.

Community
For an island family.

Oft when crowded our thoughts become
less than helpful while among,
but can arrive in forms of many

that lift us up in knowing

that those the many are there for us
and there are those that live in lack

of any.

For in those riches of being loved
we may be prone to thoughts of going
but illusions vanished in the rain

were never there

enough to remain.
Only in the hardship of the certain
that unerring presence
to spread and soften

some sense of pain.

Three Sisters

Three sisters walk the forest
together in the dawn of years
and quiet presence of the gift.
As they go they scarce to leave a trace,
and yet they wander still
in vines that reach
and seeds that burst with songs
of fervent hope for just season's falls.

In the Trees

That eucalyptus does not belong here
any more than a name no longer used
for shade.

The wind still knows the surface
of its leaves, just as well
as does the light remember
in the nightfall
the curvature of how it left.

Not over now,
still living and blown elsewhere
walking under trees that
do not move themselves
but give life in the happenstance of shadows
free of darkness.

If you think of trees as weeds
or weeds as malice,
not but the hues of decay
shall appear in the woodlands.

The birds will take their notes away
and beyond the hills of seasons
never to be heard from
toward the migrations without return.

And yet that tall and quiet torpor
stands there still today
for reasons so many that even
if culled can't ever disappear,
for the birds still sometimes sing

among its former present
canopy and will recall
to remind us gentle formerly.

The Compass

At perigee remains apprehension
that in the closest orbits
a danger lingers between suspended,
and in the friction of such crossing paths,

a withering envelops
that entangles even distant abigen
flying ever on the asterism's wings
and chrysoar draws the blade
and epsilon flees in startled flight
toward hippocrene for solace in
compassion for the falling
bellerophon, desirous in such infamy.

For in that closeness often enmity
the night sky still and calm,
always moving as one view
of components that rely on friends
and strangers to belong.

Zodiakos kyklos all in the dark forest
growing dim as apricity rounds the bend,
reunited in the morning birdsong.

The word within a language
that unifies the choir
of farflung battles raging inside.

Knowing though that surfaces
of bodies on the spin are simply useful
shells of permeable withins.

Stardust composes music
that dwells between the ears
reminding us that passion has no master
in each vast universe embraced.

Feather Boa

Should the shoulders hunch
but not simply as a shrug
yet to be released from
determined slow constriction.

Next the wings to follow
and spread out in the light
the lengthy body tightens
on and unaware of friction.

Scales of freedom's wait
in the air of hurried flight
the bird ascends beyond escape
laughing songs to deaf
and empty ears in knots
of hunger, no small degree of malice

the need to only hold the dead no benefit from the disregard
in imposition.

Fallen Water

That dry leaf that drifts turning
to the trunk and landing dry
might land on a chance
to find the imposition
of some distant lake.

Did that ascertain the weight
of the gesture from the wind
that holds such wanton skill.

The Cuts

So many cuts that that had no entry
and induced no pain at all
but hovered there as in between
the flesh of skin and mind.

Walking through the flashing steel
of unsaid risk forestalled,
no armor can protect
against the battle fought
but cognition's even keel.

Slip the thrust and weave a path
to anchor in a bay,
where becalmed we rest
to eye a peak up yonder,
calling out to climb another day.

An Ally

Deign to ask why there must still
be a war fought so many times and won before
over condescencion by aspirational superiors
wearing masks of faces of just that lost.

Some sun spun as the yarns of acquisition
during cyclone days
of yesteryear switchbacks
and latter offramps to life
called emblems of gone bust
for the reproachment providing comfort
to some fools trained solely to believe
that history belongs to the present
as if a gift from some bottomless pocket
of slander freed of discourse, or due considerative
thoughts; so to a call to friends,

or even just a simple gesture of respect
that together lift the voices of crowds
in unison to the skies that battle
pitched on faces can only ever be one
in the minds of those that still sing
the bitter tunes alone and the many
hearing peace in cheers

that invoke questions
of provision for all parts' harmonies.

The Lifecycle of the Dahlia

For the gardeners and the blooms of fog and summer.

Asleep to time and that entails
a cellar, for stunted roots of waiting
on a word forming element
that presents all spheres of history to axcan
rather than against some inherent one.

Acocoxochitl on heaves
up and through that soil
to present a future garden
that in this form
appears a barren graveyard in reverse.

Soon the cirrus begin to form
from the green below, then water canes
and wooden crutches that reach
beyond sight to rejoin a vanished
family that speaks of silent displays
of wondrous geometry and color without blue.

Not of a face or personhood of sky
withdrawn by refraction of the moment
but a beauty formed by careful
and devoted solely to enduring creation
to know and remember from afar.

Land based anemone farms
built on all the strands
from unaided in the altitudes
to domesticated fantasies of vision.

And with all thus the ability to know
that within these flowers rests

that in each and every,
the commons exist along the wild siblings still,
and so shared by all who wish to see.

Comingled time the place explodes in varied clouds
hued by the palettes of the sun
that reflect the ability to know
of the simple value of temporal perfection
that withers and sleeps then grows
over to do it all again
for just the pleasure of behold.

The Sound of the Latch

Atoms are quiet in their attempts, at eating
wonder flour, wrapped in cellophane with a purpose.
They devote themselves to both
there and still arriving behind some phalanx
of overtures that seek within seconds
levity,
look up etymology of abbreviated,
on their own.
Heard a gate close for the last time
and the physics of leaving still there
or the bad air of some mountain valley
angered, by some travel pathed
with eithers,
some stayed and fought as louder
in front of young eyes shedding wet venom
not their own.
Their own keys opened front doors
to silent afternoons
and televisions
until the nightly old eruptions
spitting older still resentments
of moments that as mere notes
as ignored write
of loss so shrill they vibrate
mountains in the distant smog
into prayers that hold
but as flimsy memories of raised on simply trying.

The Spines
On that bookstore and the folks who listen, read and walk the aisles.

All that they have seen and heard
over the spans of centuries and days,
the nights of silence within the tomes
and reflective pages on the orb
of dark until the mornings.

The titles' shifting choices made
and swallowed with rapidity
or to languish on a different shelf
or table under more,
waiting on shaded benches in a park.

Stacks of frank reminders about
compressed ages and the sign of a conception
that revolutions on a page coexist
with actions from afar, remind
that lines come to fruition in a pen
or type freed of content still

remain a protest as default
of setting ink to paper
as an act of revolt from the crouching under
and most often posthumous adulation
become the sole reward to readers,
or listeners in chairs.

And notes that call to traditions
made of pain recovered to a celebration
of sustain on community as a stage of years
established by some myriad of spokes

that refuse to nab the misdirection of said content and circled
fifths of mirrors that see and listen
that hover above the fray of wind
and hide strings and minds as suasion wielded
against the fraught and horrid display
of lives spent ever in contingency.

With sincerest gratitude to:

Wikipedia.com
Etymonline.com
Freethesaurus.com

About the Author

Having arrived at the craft later in life, David
Hutchinson feels compelled to keep on writing.
Growing up in the suburbs of a town in Southern
California declared the smoggiest in the country, he
now enjoys considering his work wandering the
milder climes of San Francisco, a respiring of a
different sort. Aside from this collection of poetry,
he has completed a work of short stories and
continues work on a second novel and a musical play.
Poetry remains more often than not.

To purchase *Sherds of Merit*
and a variety of other books, please visit

www.apsssf.com